ACKNOWLEDGEMENT

CW01646508

It has been acknowledged with deep and sincere gratitude towards Vichar Samiti that provided with this wonderful opportunity. Vichar Samiti, an esteemed NGO working for the overall development and empowerment of lives in rural as well as urban areas through 360-degree development across Health, Education, Employment, Healthcare and Sanitation. Our aim is to create a model for sustainable development that can be replicated and scaled up across the nation and globally. Our strategy is not just to create awareness, but to inspire people to improve their lives by building their confidence through a network of people who are connected by love and trust. It is through such networks that we aim to connect people and help change lives.

Special thanks to Akanksha Malaiya, Bhuvnesh Soni, Vanshikha Mahana, for their utmost support and constant guidance which abundantly helped in the accomplishment of this task. It could have been possible only through valuable learning from them which enhanced the consistency of the work profoundly.

Last but not the least, we would also like to thank friends and family for their love and support expressing it through words of encouragement and perseverance in our efforts to achieve this task.

TABLE OF CONTENTS

INTRODUCTION TO EDUCATION

Education is a planned activity with certain goals in mind, such as knowledge transmission or the development of skills and character. These objectives might include the growth of comprehension, reason, kindness, and honesty. For the purpose of separating education from indoctrination, numerous studies emphasise the importance of critical thinking. The original purpose of education was to pass on cultural heritage to future generations. Today's educational objectives increasingly include novel concepts like learner liberation, modern social skills, empathy, and sophisticated vocational abilities. There are movements for education reforms, such as those for evidence-based educational approaches or enhancing the quality and effectiveness of education in order to make it more relevant to students' lives and effective at solving problems for the present or future society as a whole. Some states and the United Nations have acknowledged the right to an education. For instance, January 24th is recognised as International Day of Education.

The field of study known as "education" is focused on how to best educate and learn in settings similar to schools. Education can be seen as the dissemination of a society's values and collective wisdom. It is comparable to what social scientists refer to as socialisation or enculturation in this regard. However, as societies become more complex, the amount of knowledge that needs to be passed down to the following generation exceeds what any one person can know, necessitating the development of more efficient and selective systems of cultural transmission. The result is formal education, which is provided by the school and the specialist known as the teacher.

By arming people with knowledge, education allows them to experience a world of opportunities. It is the promotion of learning in a variety of contexts. In the larger scheme of things, education is the process of fostering discovery and invention. Creating a movement in education where people generate their own solutions with outside assistance based on the customised curriculum is the goal of education, not coming up with solutions. Wealth, equality, humanity, and peace can all be attained via education and still are. Education is thought to help integration and emancipation, put an end to prejudice and discrimination, and address future difficulties.

TEACHING, EDUCATION AND NEW TECHNOLOGIES

[1]BHUVNESH SONI, [2] AKANKSHA MALAVIA, [3]VANSHIKHA MAHANA, [4] RHYTHM

[1,2,3]VICHAR SAMITI https://vicharsamiti.in/ INDIA
Email: [1]bhuvneshvrm@gmail.com , [2]akanksha.malaiya@gmail.com, [3]vanshikhamahana@gmail.com

Abstract: In the process of personalizing learning, technology gives students control over their own learning processes, makes learning relevant to their digital lives, and helps them prepare for the future. Students are motivated to develop as problem solvers, critical thinkers, collaborators, and creators thanks to technology and access to resources outside of the classroom. Students who experience excellent classroom technology integration grow to love learning for the rest of their lives. Technology in education and having the correct gadgets in kids' hands helps them prepare for the professional and technical skills they will need to be successful now and in the workforce of the future. Relevant STEAM learning experiences can spark creativity, assist students in applying meaning to their learning, and prepare them for future career prospects and employment that have yet to be formed. Coding, programming, physical computing, and computational thinking skills have all grown commonplace in the workforce. Students can learn these skills while also developing their problem-solving and logical abilities for the twenty-first century through making.
"Technology is nothing. What's important is that you have faith in the people that use it, that they're basically good and smart, and if you give them tools, they'll do wonderful things with them."

Keywords: Technology, critical thinkers, STEAM learning, problem-solving

WHAT EXACTLY DO WE MEAN WHEN WE SAY "TECHNOLOGY"?

The term "technology" refers to improvements in the ways and tools we employ to solve problems or achieve our objectives. Technology in the classroom might include everything from a low-tech pencil, paper, and chalkboard to presentation software, iPads, internet collaboration and conferencing tools, and more.
The most recent technology enable us to do things in physical and virtual classrooms that were previously impossible. What you employ is ultimately determined by your objectives.
Technology empowers students on the way to personalising learning by providing them control over how they study, making education relevant to their digital lives, and preparing them for their futures. Students are driven to become problem solvers, critical thinkers, collaborators, and creators as a result of technology and access to resources outside of the classroom. Students develop a lifetime love of learning when technology is skilfully integrated into classrooms.

Educators are constantly working to tailor learning for their students. With access to real-time student data, longitudinal statistics, material, apps, and more, technology may help them reach new heights. Technology may assist educators in creating blended learning environments and leveraging digital tools for formative and summative assessments, introducing new learning and teaching methods into classrooms.

TEACHING WITH TECHNOLOGY

Teaching with technology can deepen student learning by supporting instructional objectives. However, choosing the "greatest" tech tools while keeping your student learning goals in mind might be difficult. Once those tools have been found, incorporating them might be a difficulty, albeit an eye-opening experience.

Technology in education and having the correct gadgets in kids' hands helps them prepare for the professional and technical skills they will need to be successful now and in the workforce of the future. Relevant STEAM learning experiences can spark creativity, assist students in applying meaning of their learning, and prepare them for future career prospects and employment that have yet to be formed. Coding, programming, physical computing, and computational thinking skills have all grown commonplace in the workforce. Students can learn these skills and enhance their problem-solving and critical thinking abilities through creation. When designed and linked with the correct technologies, learning by doing with maker mindsets and surroundings can be incredibly engaging.

WHAT ROLE DOES TECHNOLOGY PLAY IN YOUR LIFE?

- Online collaboration technologies, such as those found in Google Apps, enable students and instructors to share documents, modify them in real time, and project them on a screen. This provides students with a collaborative platform for brainstorming ideas and documenting their work with text and photographs.
- Presentation software (such as PowerPoint) allows instructors to include high-resolution pictures, diagrams, films, and sound files in addition to text and verbal lecture content.
- Tablets may be linked to computers, projectors, and the cloud, allowing students and instructors to communicate via text, drawings, and diagrams.
- • Canvas, for instance, allows instructors to manage all of the
- materials learners need for a course (e.g., syllabus, tasks, books, practice tests), provide excellent grading tools, and create spaces for debate, document sharing, and video and audio commentary. Canvas webpages are automatically allocated to all courses.
- Clickers and cell phones make it simple to survey pupils in class. This is ideal for rapid polling, which allows instructors to quickly assess students' understanding and change pace and material.
- Lecture-capture software, such as Panopto, enables instructors to record lectures straight from their computer, eliminating the need for elaborate or additional classroom equipment. Consider recording your lectures as you deliver them and then posting them online for students to watch again. According to research, posting taped lectures does not reduce attendance, and students value the option to examine lectures at their own leisure.

LEARNING ON ONE'S OWN HAS GROWN SIMPLER AND MORE EFFECTIVE.

You may find information in any field on the internet. Whatever you need to know, you can readily get it online. Although the facts and the source cannot always be trusted, they can nevertheless be used as educational materials. Students can access the internet without the help of teachers or parents.

Many students become preoccupied with other activities and fail to focus on their tasks. Many students use writing services to have experienced writers compose their academic papers. When kids learn on their own, they must accept responsibility when they make mistakes. In such cases, hiring a writing service is vital.

Because website content and electronic books are continuously updated, learners can readily obtain up-to-date information. Even if they do not attend classes, students can learn a lot.

EDUCATION AND MODERN TECHNOLOGIES

According to the most recent findings regarding how current students of today choose to use technology and how technology affects their learning, it was discovered that the usage of new equipment technology and tools promotes student learning and interactivity. When technology is used, they find it lot more interactive and full of exciting places. Knowledge transfer becomes extremely simple, convenient, and effective. What this indicates is that our minds today prefer to operate faster when supported by contemporary technology, be it in any aspect of life, in this case schooling.

The dependence and reliance on such an innovation, which simply makes life easier and smoother, is completely inescapable these days, even in schools, colleges, and academic institutions. Today's students can use technology in the following areas:

Internet access and continuous connectivity. Over the last decade, the internet has expanded in importance by orders of magnitude. Its significance in the realm of education can no longer be overstated. Despite the risks of fraud and other downsides, the internet is a boon to students. The internet is now present in practically all of the products we use. The internet is virtually everywhere, from television to video game consoles to our devices.

The internet provides students with incredible ease; they can obtain numerous types of help, tutorials, and other types of assisting material that may be used to academically develop and enhance their learning. Making use of projectors and images. When compared to words, visual images always have a stronger attraction. Another excellent application of technology is the use of projectors and images to aid with learning. Top colleges throughout the world are now relying on excellent PowerPoint presentations and projections to keep studying alive and exciting. Using technology such as projectors in schools and colleges can increase interaction and interest while also improving motivation.

The educational sector's digital footprint

When it comes to digital and education, the penetration of digital media in the education sector has increased. This penetration has resulted in around-the-clock interaction with students and many forums that are available for various types of tasks or aid. As the power of digital grows, there are and will be more applications that will aid kids in their development and learning.

Technology-enabled online degrees

Online degrees have now become a very typical occurrence. People want to attend online courses for learning and certification. Top colleges provide wonderful online programmes that make use of diverse tools and the internet.

This is a concept that will gain traction as more people support and become aware of it. The online degree scenario is becoming increasingly popular among students who work and seek flexible learning options around the world.

The significance of technology in education

The role of technology in education is fourfold: it is included as part of the curriculum, as an instructional delivery system, as a way of assisting instructions, and as a tool to enhance the entire learning process.

Education has evolved from passive and reactive to participatory and aggressive as a result of technological advancements.

Education is critical in both corporate and academic environments. In the former, education or training is utilised to assist workers in doing things differently than they did previously. In the latter, education is oriented toward instilling curiosity in pupils' minds. In any situation, the use of technology can improve students' understanding and retention of concepts.

POSITIVE INFLUENCE

1. Improved Teaching and Learning:

- Technological advancements such as digital cameras, projectors, mind training software, computers, Power Point presentations, and 3D visualisation tools have all become valuable resources for teachers in assisting students in readily grasping a topic.
- It must be realised that visual explanations of concepts make learning entertaining and pleasurable for kids. They are able to participate more in class, and professors are given the opportunity to make their classes more dynamic and fascinating.

2. Globalization:

- When kids attend school in different parts of the state, they can "meet" their counterparts via video conferencing without leaving the classroom.
- Some websites, such as www.glovico.com, assist students in learning foreign languages online by matching a group of students with a teacher from another nation.

3. No Geographical Restrictions:

- With the development of online degree programmes, there is little requirement to be physically present in the classroom.
- Several foreign colleges have also launched online degree programmes that students can enrol in.
- Distance learning and online education are becoming an integral element of the educational system.

HARMFUL EFFECT

1. Writing abilities are deteriorating.

- The writing skills of today's young generation have suffered greatly as a result of their overuse of internet chatting and shortcuts.

- Children nowadays are so reliant on digital communication that they have completely forgotten about honing their writing skills.
- They don't know how to spell different words, how to use grammar correctly, or how to write in cursive.

2. Increasing Cheating Incidents:
   - Technological advancements such as graphical calculators, high-tech watches, tiny cameras, and similar devices have become excellent sources of exam cheating.
   - It is easier for pupils to scribble calculations and notes on graphing calculators since they are less likely to be caught.

3. Inattention:
   - SMS or text texting has become a popular pastime among many students.
   - Students can be observed playing with their cell phones or iPhones at all hours of the day and night, as well as while driving and, very often, in between lectures.
   - Being constantly connected to the internet world has resulted in a lack of attention and concentration in academics and, to a lesser extent, sports and extracurricular activities.

BENEFITS

- It increases kids' motivation to learn.
- Allow students with hectic schedules to work from home on their own time.
- Train pupils to gain new technology abilities that they can apply in the workplace afterwards.
- Reduce paper and photocopying costs while promoting the "green revolution" notion.

DISADVANTAGES

- Many professionals and experienced people believe that such technology in education reduces pupils' imagination and thinking abilities.
- It might also be time demanding from the standpoint of the teacher.
- It is expensive to install such technology, and there may be health risks if used excessively.

EMERGING TECHNOLOGIES THAT WILL IMPACT EDUCATION IN 2022.

When it comes to developing technologies in our world today, the list appears to be virtually endless. Technology has altered our perspective of the world. With new types of unique technology arriving every year, we should not be surprised to observe significant changes in numerous corners of the world. Education is no different.
Education is an essential component of any community. As a student, you may encounter obstacles from time to time. Fortunately, outstanding tools have been developed to assist

individuals in overcoming their obstacles. For example, Canadian students can always acquire Canadian academic help from well-known solutions designed just for them.

Learning has never been easier since the advent of digital platforms. The following is a list of emerging technologies that will impact education in 2022.

Emerging technologies in education all have the same goal: to revolutionise the learning process for pupils. These technologies promise to improve the way teachers and students work. And with such technology dominating our modern world, education is bound to change.

We'll need to take a closer look at each one to give you a clearer idea of which upcoming technologies will help reshape education in 2022. Here's how it works:

1. **Simulations with Augmented Reality (AR)**

Augmented Reality and Simulations have made an impact on the visual world. Today, its widespread influence has begun to shape how students study and engage with their teachers.

AR has been around for a while. However, due to its ever-evolving nature, it is regarded as one of the world's most promising emergent technologies. According to studies on AR and education, it is expected to have a significant impact on how education is perceived by 2022.

Augmented Reality claims to be the finest technique to capture humans' dreams and fantasies. And by 2022, it promises to assist students in capturing such imaginations in order to improve their learning process.

2. **Learning that adapts**

Adaptive learning, as the name implies, is a technology that gives learning activities to students based on their needs and learning style/behaviour. Consider adaptive learning to be a piece of technology that quickly adapts to each student's demands. It assists pupils in adapting to distinct learning routes that are fully based on their interests and learning abilities.

Technology research has shown that it will play a significant part in the world's educational system in 2022. The system can be altered by its presence since it orchestrates the interaction with the learner using computer algorithms. Although adaptive learning was inspired by artificial intelligence, it continues to actively deliver tailored resources as well as top learning activities.

The principal application of adaptive learning is in the sphere of education. However, the technology was also designed to help business trainers deliver more effective business training. Considering the rate of advancement, technology is seen as one of several that will transform education in the year 2022.

3. **Technology in Education Using Artificial Intelligence (AI)**

Artificial intelligence is often recognised as one of the world's most hotly debated technological trends. The globe has come to trust its technology in its development because of its sensible approach to numerous systems. AI, while employed in a variety of sectors, is not confined to education. In further depth, its existence has aided the evolution of the world, and fortunately, by 2022, education will have progressed to new levels.

AI will transform schooling by 2022. It is most likely to accomplish this via facilitating the dissemination of first-person perspectives. This can be useful when students are working on essays, term papers, or research papers about a specific culture or tradition.

For example, Google bot and most search bots will attempt to read a brief summary from an online search. However, there is a better scenario in which stories from first-hand sources are shared. And this is what AI aspires to be.

4. Application of 5G Technologies in Education

The fifth generation of wireless technology is known as 5G. Anyone who uses it can benefit from high speed and low latency wireless technology thanks to its upgraded upgrades. Students are more likely to profit from this one-of-a-kind invention because it promises faster downloads of student files and resources as well as more powerful networks.

Suggestions for the unique qualities that 5G can offer to education by 2022 have been made. One example is a hologram teacher who may facilitate talks on specific topics. Another hypothesis is that students can benefit more from distance learning and virtual reality experiences.

5. Robotics

A large part of the world we live in is driven by automation. As engagement rises, business and economic sectors employ automation to provide better, faster experiences. The school sector would undoubtedly gain from automation features by 2022.

Students have a better probability of obtaining lectures at precise times using automation. Lectures can be arranged digitally. Not to mention that automation makes it easier to incorporate the use of artificial intelligence.

6. Education Based on Competencies

People should expect competency-based education to play an important part in the educational system by 2022. Students are matched with learning activities that are appropriate for their level of learning capacity thanks to this unique technology. To put it another way, competency-based education allows students to enhance their learning experience based on their ability to master a skill. This enables pupils to learn at their own pace, independent of their surroundings.

Students can efficiently give improved outcomes through competency-based education. It aids in the measurement of outcomes that are solely dependent on a student's objective demonstration of competency in a certain area.

7. Analytics for Learning

Learning is a comprehensive process that necessitates effective tracking and analysis in order to better understand outcomes. Learning analytics, as a new technology, is currently being utilised by teachers to better record students' learning behaviours.

Another distinct advantage of tracking student learning rates and behaviours is that most teachers will be able to provide targeted adjustments to courses. In education, improvement is a critical aspect that enhances each student's learning experience. This is what learning analytics may assist teachers in providing to their students. Fortunately, by 2022, this will be a widely used technology.

CONCLUSION

To summarise, several upcoming technologies are poised to significantly reshape education. By researching each of the following technologies, students may make better use of them. By researching each one, users gain unique insights into how to get the most out of their usage. Teachers, on the other hand, can employ online course platforms to improve the learning environment.

This paper aims to accomplish this by providing crucial technological facts. As a student, you should be willing to embrace technology in order to improve your learning experience.

REFERENCE:

https://www.inc.com/marcel-schwantes/steve-jobs-once-said-that-technology-is-nothing-heres-what-is-more-important-thank-goodness.html

https://www.qemsolutions.com/news/technology-is-nothing

https://blog.ezygo.app/a-guide-to-teaching-with-technology/

https://www.sciencedirect.com/topics/computer-science/modern-technology

https://itchronicles.com/education/modern-technology-in-education/

https://www.thehansindia.com/life-style/impact-of-modern-technology-on-education-712457

https://www.researchgate.net/publication/325086709_Impact_of_modern_technology_in_education

https://baronmag.ca/2019/07/advantages-and-disadvantages-of-modern-technology-in-students-life/

TEACHING AND LEARNING WITH TECHNOLOGY: EFFECTIVENESS OF INTEGRATING ICT WITH CLASSROOM PEDAGOGY

[1]BHUVNESH SONI, [2] AKANKSHA MALAVIA, [3]VANSHIKHA MAHANA [4]PARNEET KAUR

[1,2,3] VICHAR SAMITI https://vicharsamiti.in/ INDIA

[1,2,3]VICHAR SAMITI https://vicharsamiti.in/ INDIA

Email: [1]bhuvneshvrm@gmail.com , [2]akanksha.malaiya@gmail.com, [3]vanshikhamahana@gmail.com [4]kaurparneet2004@gmail.com

Abstract

The explosive rise of ICT over the last two decades and specially during COVID – 19 , has elevated it to the top of the list of educational researchers' hot-button issues. This is a result of ICT's capacity to offer a lively and proactive teaching and learning environment. Integration of information, communication, and technology (ICT) into pedagogy will help teachers meet the global need for substituting technology-based teaching and learning tools and facilities for traditional teaching techniques. ICT is regarded as one of the key components in preparing the nation for future development. The New Education Policy (NEP 2020) incorporates technology-based teaching and learning as an important part of the national curriculum for schools. The purpose of this study is to examine instructors' opinions of how well ICT integration supports the teaching and learning process. Additionally, the effectiveness of ICT integration in education is the chief topic of this article. In more detail, this paper tries to assess problems faced by teachers and administrators in integrating ICT into their active pedagogies.

Keywords: ICT , Integration, Teaching-Learning, Education,

A. Introduction

The phrase "technology" is a significant concern in many disciplines, including education, in the twenty-first century. This is because in most nations, technology has replaced traditional means of knowledge sharing. The way people think, work, and live has completely changed as a result of breakthroughs and the transformation of our societies brought about by technology integration today. This calls for schools and other educational institutions to take into account integrating ICT into their curricula in order to prepare students for living in "a knowledge society" (Ghavifekr, Afshari & Amla Salleh, 2012).

The use of computer-based communication that is integrated into the regular educational process in the classroom is referred to as information, communication, and technology (ICT) integration in education. Teachers are viewed as the essential players in implementing ICT in their regular classroom settings and training pupils for the contemporary digital environment. This is a result of ICT's ability to provide an active and dynamic teaching-learning environment (Arnseth & Hatlevik, 2012). The goal of ICT integration is to enhance and raise the quality, accessibility, and cost-efficiency of how education is delivered to students, but it also refers to the advantages of networking learning communities to meet the problems of present globalization

B. Pedagogy Design and ICT

The main factors influencing the effectiveness of learning are: Educational design for effective use of ICT. Instead of embedding the curriculum in the computer, the computer should be embedded in the curriculum. Effective ICT integration should therefore focus on educational design by justifying how and why the technology is used in this way. Effective ICT integration into the learning process has the potential to increase learner motivation (Wang & Woo, 2007). Teachers should be encouraged to incorporate ICT into their lessons. They need to recognize the effectiveness of ICT in facilitating learners' learning. School administrators can play an important role in promoting her ICT integration to enhance the government's implementation of her ICT programs.

C. Three main stages for ICT to be highly valued and regarded by the teachers

The three main stages of ICT adoption—integration, enhancement, and complementary—have been identified by Hermans, Tondeur, Van-Braak, and Valcke (2008). The goal of the integration approach is to increase student achievement and attainment by implementing appropriate ICT use in a specific subject area that calls for complex concepts and skills. Additionally, a review of the curriculum is required to ensure that only pertinent ICT resources and suitable software are installed in order to accomplish the primary goals and objectives of the curriculum. The enhancement strategy involves heavily emphasising the introduced issue utilising ICT. Microsoft PowerPoint, for instance, can be used to present the subject in a highly unique and imaginative style that will encourage conversation and the exchange of ideas and views. Lastly, complementary method is when the ICT is used to assist and back the pupil‘s education. This strategy enables students to be more productive and organised by allowing them to take notes on a computer, submit their work via email from home as long as the deadline is met, and look up material from a variety of internet sources to complete the assignment assigned to them.

D. Importance of ICT Integration in School Pedagogy

Numerous studies have demonstrated that ICT integration effectively gives students a wealth of. Many nations have recently recognised the value of ICT education and training for citizens with the necessary skills to access information and take part in transactions through these technologies. ICT provides the tools for creating, collecting, storing, using, and attaining knowledge through communication and collaboration (Kozma, 2003). (Kozma, 2008).

According to a number of studies, using ICT in education has the potential to enhance current methods of teaching and learning. In addition, Zang and Aikman (2007) found computer education has increased students' interest in education which has an impact on their enrolment, attendance, retention, level of motivation, and achievement; Chou's (2003) observed ICT is seen as a tool to revolutionise education, improve learner engagement, and increase student achievement. Kubiatko (2013) found that effective use of technology can motivate students, make classes more dynamic and interesting, and renew teacher enthusiasm as they learn new skills and techniques; Unwin (2009) argued that ICT can act as a catalyst by giving users tools that help them become better teachers and by allowing students access to electronic media that help make concepts more understandable and accessible. He also demonstrated that ICT is viewed as a key tool in enhancing performance, collaboration, learning, experience, and learning outcomes. ICT has quickly emerged as one of the fundamental pillars of contemporary society, as noted by UNESCO in 2002. To ensure that all nations—developed and developing—have access to the best educational resources required to equip children with the skills they need to participate fully in contemporary society and to contribute to a knowledge-based society, UNESCO encouraged member countries to adopt ICT-based pedagogy. Many nations today value comprehension and mastery.

E. The Potential Benefits of ITC Integration in school pedagogy

ICT can provide a considerable benefit in supporting learning. Students can learn actively if they use technology in their studies. They will be aware of the information they require, the reasons why they require it, and the methods by which they can obtain it. Rendering Bransford, Brown, and Cocking (quoted in Huffaker, 2003, p. 357), active learning gives students the freedom to choose when they need to know a certain piece of knowledge and whether they already comprehend it or not.

An independent learning is implied by this active learning. Students who have access to the internet in class will no longer be completely dependent on their instructors. They can search through the information on the internet, copy the information they need, and continue searching for new data.

Students that use this learning approach also learn to manage their own learning. Self-managed learning enables students to be self-motivated and self-directed learners who will be able to readily, efficiently, and swiftly adapt to the sudden change in knowledge. For instance, using a blog helps keep educators and students very current on topics and discussions in the educational sector or other sectors.

ICT can also offer a platform for interactive and group learning. Our ability to learn is not constrained by the hours we spend in school, our location, or the characteristics of our teachers thanks to the internet. We have access to the internet everywhere, at any time. E-learning enables students to access material more quickly from any location at any time.

Technology also helps us to transcend demographic boundaries. Rural students have access to information from urban regions, can learn from other students or professors in the same region or even in other countries, and can exchange knowledge with them. In addition to enabling dynamic learning, ICT enables all of the school's human staff members—principals, administrators, instructors, IT coordinators, and students—to participate in cooperative learning and create learning communities.

Interactivity and communication are the most crucial aspects of collaborative learning that we seek to accomplish with ICT. Effective learning occurs when pupils are interactively engaged in a learning task, according to Rodrigues (2002, pp. 134–135). ICT-based education goes beyond memorization-based education. It enables students to engage in active learning, enjoy using technology, and have fun while doing so.

ICT can help us learn metacognitively. We can learn how to learn rather than just a certain skill by incorporating ICT in our learning, as mentioned by Monteith (quoted in Monteith, 2002, p. 21). This enables us to see that acquiring new technology and information is not more challenging than learning existing knowledge and skills. This knowledge is crucial since many people are reluctant to learn new technology because they believe that learning something new is more complicated and challenging than acquiring an existing skill.

F. Difficulties to Integrate ICT into Educational Institution and Pedagogy

Because it is such a multifaceted process, integrating ICT into teaching and learning may be difficult. Using a variety of different classification frameworks, researchers and educators have divided the problems with ICT use in educational institutions into extrinsic and intrinsic categories.

Access, time, support, resources, and training were listed as first-order extrinsic problem characteristics by Ertmer, while second-order internal problem characteristics included attitude, beliefs, practises, and resistance. Hendren, however, believed that institutions rather than people were the source of extrinsic difficulties, while teachers, administrators, and individuals were the focus of intrinsic issues.

A different viewpoint characterises the physical and psychological circumstances that prevent ICT use in educational institutions as hurdles

The lack of sufficient computers and software copies could be the material condition. The non-material barriers include instructors' inadequate ICT knowledge and abilities, the challenge of incorporating ICT in instruction, and a lack of teacher time. In most schools, technical issues became a major problem, a source of frustration for students and teachers, and disrupted the teaching and learning process. Without technical support and without repairs, the teacher will be temporarily unable to use the computer. As a result, lack of subject matter support discourages teachers from using computers for fear of equipment failure. Technical problems therefore become a major obstacle for teachers. These issues include poor connectivity, virus attacks, and malfunctioning printers..

G. Conclusion

ICTs play a recurrent and inevitable role in education. Rapid technological advancements suggest that ICT will play a significant role in the future of the educational system. We may conclude from present educational activities and practises that the development of ICTs has had a significant impact on "what is learned, How it is learned, When & where learning takes place, Who is learning and who is teaching." ICT also emphasises changing the function of teachers. In addition to teaching in the classroom, they will also have other duties and talents. Teachers will serve as virtual mentors for kids who use technology. In the end, ICT use will improve kids' educational opportunities. In a world where technology is developing quickly, ICT is playing an increasingly important role in assisting students in establishing successful careers and personal lives.

BIBLIOGRAPHY

1. Zang P and Aikman S (2007) Attitudes in ICT acceptance and use. In: Jacko J (ed.) Human-Computer Interactions: Interaction Design and Usability. Berlin: Springer, pp. 1021–1030.

2. Kozma R (2003) Technology, Innovation, and Educational Change: A Global Perspective. Eugene: International Society for Technology in Education.

3. Kozma R (2008) Comparative analyses of policies for ICT in education. In: Voogt J and Knezek G (eds) International Handbook of Information Technology in Education. Berlin: Springer Science, pp. 1083–1096.

4. Kubiatko M (2013) The comparison of different age groups on the attitudes toward and the use of ICT. Educational Sciences: Theory and Practice 13(2): 1263–1272.

5. Kundu A (2018) A study on Indian teachers‘ roles and willingness to accept education technology.

6. International Journal of Innovative Studies in Sociology and Humanities (IJISSH) 3(9): 42–52. Available at: http://ijissh.org/articles/2018-2/volume-3-issue-9/ (accessed 25 August 2020).

7. Huffaker D. (2003). Reconnecting the classroom: E-learning pedagogy in US public high schools. Australian Journal of Educational Technology, 19 (3), 356-370

8. Uhomoibhi, J., O. (2006). Implementing e-learning in Northern Ireland: Prospects and challenges. Campus-Wide Information Systems, 23 (1), 4-14.

9. Rodrigues S. (2002). Opportunistic challenges. Teaching and learning with ICT. New York: Nova Science Publishers, Inc.

10. Monteith, M. (ed.) (2002). ICT: Teaching primary literacy with ICT. Buckingham: Open University Press

11. Suryani, Adi. (2010). ICT IN EDUCATION: ITS BENEFITS, DIFFICULTIES, AND ORGANIZATIONAL DEVELOPMENT ISSUES. Jurnal Sosial Humaniora.

12. Ertmer, P. (1999). Addressing first-and second-order barriers to change: Strategies for technology integration. Educational Technology Research and Development, 47(4), 47-61.

13. Ghavifekr, S., Afshari, M., & Amla Salleh. (2012). Management strategies for E-Learning system as the core component of systemic change: A qualitative analysis. Life Science Journal, 9(3), 2190-2196.

14. Arnseth, H.C., & Hatlevik, O.E. (2010). Challenges in aligning pedagogical practices and pupils‘ competencies with the Information Society‘s demands: The case of Norway. In S. Mukerji & P. Triphati (Eds.), Cases on technological adaptability and transnational learning: Issues and challenges. Hershey: IGI global.

15. Hermans, R; Tondeur, J; Van Braak, J; & Valcke, M. (2008).
The impact of primary school teachers‘ educational beliefs on the classroom use of computers. Computers & Education, 51(4), 1499-1509.

16. Wang, H. (2006). An implementation study of the English as a foreign language curriculum policies in the Chinese tertiary context. Unpublished doctoral thesis, Queen‘s University, Kingston, Ontario, Canada.

International Conference on Teaching, Education and new learning Technologies (ICTENLT)

Importance of technology in learning and teaching

[1]BHUVNESH SONI, [2] AKANKSHA MALAVIA, [3]VANSHIKHA MAHANA, [4] ANUSHKA MAHESHWARI

[1,2,3] VICHAR SAMITI https://vicharsamiti.in/ INDIA
Email: [1]bhuvneshvrm@gmail.com , [2]akanksha.malaiya@gmail.com, [3]vanshikhamahana@gmail.com , [4]21jsgp-amaheshwari@jgu.edu.in)

ABSTRACT

Today, educational technology performs a major role in the way people communicate across the world. With the help of technology, there has been an advantage in education, the ways of learning, and the way people communicate with each other. This paper provides information and knowledge about how technology has taken place in education and the learning styles across the world. It describes how educational technology is an organized process to improve the quality of education and how it has changed the teaching techniques of tutors, teachers, and educators all across the world. This paper also provides a spotlight on how the students take help of the internet when it comes to education and learning. Technology is the powerful and handiest tool. In today's era, everyone should know how to operate PowerPoint, excel, or zoom, and everyone should be familiar with the digital environment. This paper also provides a brief discussion on how the covid-19 pandemic brought changes in the way of learning and education and what the students and the educators did to overcome the barriers proposed by the covid-19 pandemic in

2020. This paper also presents a comparison between the 20th century and the 21st-century education and learning system lastly, the paper is concluded by stating the facts that technology brought upon education and learning techniques.

KEYWORDS: Educational technology, educators, Learning technology, digital education, E-learning, pandemic.

INDEX

Introduction

Education has always been a part of societies all over the world. It is the process of helping a person learn and being literate has always been proven beneficial for the people in a society. School and education are synonyms for some people as schools are a major part of education as schools help a person develop important skills like social interaction. Humans can learn, store language, and communicate with each other. In the 4th century B.C., the word school came from the Greek word _schole', the schools then were only available to the aristocracy at that time.[3] It was the Greek people who formed the primary and the secondary schools and there have been historic examples of education from the places like India, China, and parts of middle east Asia. The first tools used by the students and the teachers were for writing like clay slates. By the 1600s, the library and pencil were invented, and later in the 19th century, textbooks became available for students and teachers for learning purposes.[3] The 20th century was a very major and most important time for education in history. According to Dewey, education should be about reflective, critical thinking, and analyzing and not memorizing facts.[3] he stated this because he thought that people were mugging up the facts and the information provided to them rather than presenting reflective thinking about what they read.

In the 19th century, computer learning was developed and PLATO, an instruction system for computers was developed. Then in the mid-1980s came Artificial Intelligence (AI), AI has not been able to help education in any way whatsoever but scientists are working on it. Seymour Papert predicted that computers would help students gain ~~a~~ sense of mastery over a piece of the most modern and powerful technology and establish an intimate contact with some of the deepest ideas from science, from mathematics, and the art of intellectual model building."[4] Technology has shaped history and will always help the students and the teachers in future generations. But education and the learning techniques and system were under threat when the world entered into a crisis from which it can never recover. The covid 19 pandemic proposed a large threat to education and the learning techniques and system and here technology helped and made way through and eased the learners and the educators.

How does the covid pandemic bring changes in the learning pattern?

The spread of the pandemic in 2020 was a threat to education and the learning techniques and system and also to humankind. Covid 19 made changes and altered education and the way of learning. All the educational institutions were forced to closed and switched to E-learning. E-learning is the learning done from home through an online medium using technology. This sudden transformation from physical learning to E-learning was a difficult task to manage for students and educators all over the world and posed a threat to education and the education system. E-learning played a vital role, most students wanted to study online and graduate as they cannot go and reside in unfamiliar surroundings.

However, there were some drawbacks of E-learning like the students missed face-to-face learning experiences. The assignments which they got were limited to some objective questions that didn't provide them with enough testing. One of the challenges of E-learning was related to the misuse of technology. Students have dealt a lot during this time. There are some events like farewells, proms, athletic events, and many other social events which some students didn't even experience. There were high rates of depression and anxiety during the pandemic. According to a report, 14.4% of teenagers reported post-traumatic stress while 40.4% reported depression and anxiety. If we combine all the reports that the medical centers gathered, we will find that the pandemic brought complications to the mental health of children. An increase in social media during the pandemic led to an increase in the screen time of children. Excessive screen time is then associated with less sleep, bad habits, and mental and physical problems. While there were challenges, there were also some benefits from E-learning. Through E-learning, the students can save their travel expenses and can also save time as they don't have to go to college or school to study. Technology has made its way through many houses and schools by installing high-speed internet and computers. Through technology, the barrier was easily overcome.

A new way of learning with technology

Technology and education are synonymous and students now cannot imagine education without technology. During the pandemic time, technology has helped a lot to overcome the barrier of online learning. Computers have always been a part of the lives of the people of the world. Technology has changed how we communicate and organize our lives and due to technology we are now more informed and connected. Learning technology is a term, it is used to explain communication and information tools that are used to enhance learning and teaching. The key ingredients of Learning technology are tutorials, communication tools, and productivity tools. Tutorials are models in a structured format. It includes digital tools and media for learning and teaching. Learning technology increases the responsibility of the student. Educational technology also supports individual learning which then creates room and space for learning from one's own mistakes. The education environment is altered by technology which has made it much easier and more efficient for educators and students. Students all over the world enjoy learning more creatively and effectively with the help of technology and the guidance of educators. Many schools across the world let the students study using technology.

Technology and education weren't always synonymous. Students find learning easy with the creative ways of technology, teachers also can use the technology to adopt new learning skills. Educators also like using technology as technology eases their workload.

Teachers believed that including digital technology in the classrooms may decrease the concentration of the students over time as then the intervention would deviate them from focusing in the class. This was true as the students did get deviate from their goals and lost their focus on their studies.

However, some teachers, on the other hand, thought that digital education can bring individualization to the students as students have different capacities to learn and educate themselves, everyone is different from the other and some may even need special attention. Educational technology is a tool that helps the teachers in engaging with the students on an individual basis. That is why educational technology has helped in improving the quality of education over time.

Due to the covid pandemic in 2020, the students and the teachers were forced to do the education online using apps like Zoom or Microsoft Outlook. The education was compelled to be done in an online-based which brought hardships for students and teachers. Apart from the covid pandemic in 2020, technology in the form of the internet has always brought a positive impact on the lives of students and teachers.

Learning has become more effective and efficient through the internet as provides the students and teachers with digital books and allows them to highlight words and also make notes side by side. The teachers also have the option of creating attractive presentations and can however also conduct small online quizzes to grasp what students have learned throughout, they can also acquire useful feedback from the students.

In today's era, everyone should know how to operate PowerPoint, Excel, or zoom, and everyone should be familiar with the digital environment. Students can also learn hearing audio and video tools.

New technology may be exciting for some and traumatizing for some. Students need guidance when it comes to dealing with unfamiliar and strange technologies and may need assistance from their teachers so that they don't deviate from their goals and don't lose focus. The schools should also provide solutions to improve learning. Through technology, teachers can explain new concepts and ideas but the introduction of new technologies will also change how a teacher teaches. Usage of technology is motivational for the pupils. It has the potential to improve feedback and also increased the accuracy of the assignment which then reduces the decision-making time and workload for the teacher. The teacher can use technology to track the progress over time. Usage of technology increases flexibility. The teachers benefit from the technology when it comes to assessment. The teachers can make PowerPoint make the classroom more creative and differentiated from other teachers. They can also search the internet for new concepts to make their presentations more informative. Digital technologies can make things and learning much easier and more effective. Technology has changed education, the ways educators teach, and the way students learn. Technology is a large part of the classrooms, digital technology is used to create experiences that will benefit the ways educators teach and the way students learn.

Comparison of the 20th century and the 21st-century education and learning system

If we compare the 20th century and the 21st-century education and learning system then we will know that there have been many modifications done and the quality of education has improved. The students now can learn many things and courses only at a reasonable price. However, the students in the 20th century were dependent on the local people and the books available in the library. The Internet has made things easy and efficient for teachers and students. The Internet has given education a new and creative form. the teachers and the students now have access to unlimited information and tools. the students in the 20th century could not afford books as they were expensive for the masses. But now in the 21st century, books are available for free on the internet through technology. The students do not have to carry heavy books like in the 20th century, they can simply download the e-books on their portable devices and carry their portable devices with them. E-books have minimized the cost of education. In the 20th century, teacher assistance was only limited to the classroom and the schools but in the 21st century, teachers are now available on social media platforms and the students can easily seek advice from them there. The students of the past will never know how nowadays students study with the help of technology, they will never know how to make effective PowerPoint presentations or use the internet for studies and learning. Back in the 20th century, students had no other option than to learn from school physically, but in the 21st century, the internet provides many courses online at an affordable price. The internet also provides attractive and creative ways for learning.

Conclusion

One cannot escape the fact that technology is in everybody's pocket from a 3-year-old to a 58 years old grown-up man. Technology is everywhere. Around 16% of 8 to 11-year-olds own more than five media devices.[2] In 2011, 7% of 3-15 children owned a table which has increased to 51% in 2016.[2] Technology means that the students of today have information that the students of the past did not have. Computers have evolved massively and computing has been made affordable to the masses. Then BBC micro became a hit in education. Computers have transformed the whole world, offices, homes, and schools, and have also made education more easier and efficient.

Back in the 19th and the 20th century, the quality of education depended on different schools however it is not the same today. The presence of technology is growing gradually in the classroom, the internet provides many creative and advanced courses to students. The schools have IT lessons in the schools, but they are taught what they already know in these lessons. Technology in schools is a distraction for the students as the lecture gets a little boring, they text underneath the table and lose their focus on the topic being taught in the class, it distracts them from the education and takes away valuable and important lesson time. Educational technology has always been around since the beginning of schooling in the USA, with paper, pencils, and slates, but what has changed over the last 2 decades has been that we have moved from a whole group activity to personalizing and individualizing instruction through technology. Students can be using the same software but can be doing very different things with it like painting, coloring, etc based on their interests and levels. The teachers should think, _what is it that they want to teach, and is there a better way to teach using technology.[1] The teachers use technology so that they can make the students understand in a better way, they are also using many new technologies in the classrooms but some of them need special techniques to master technology.

References

1. (18161) How Is Technology Transforming Teaching & Classrooms? | Learning Upgrade: Technology in Iowa Schools - YouTube

2. (18166) Redefining Learning & Teaching using Technology. | Jason Brown | TEDxNorwichED - YouTube
3. A Brief History of Education (& Educational Technology) - Technology for Learners
4. The Evolution of Learning Technologies | InformED (opencolleges.edu.au)
5. The Effect of COVID-19 on Education - PMC (nih.gov)

New National Education Policy 2020: Concepts, Approaches, and Challenges

[1]BHUVNESH SONI, [2] AKANKSHA MALAVIA, [3]VANSHIKHA MAHANA, [4] SWARNALATA WANKHEDE

[1,2,3]VICHAR SAMITI https://vicharsamiti.in/ INDIA
Email: [1]bhuvneshvrm@gmail.com , [2]akanksha.malaiya@gmail.com, [3]vanshikhamahana@gmail.com

Abstract

Education is a virtue a person may carry with them all their life. Collectively, educated people are any country's think tanks, development engines, and conscience guardians. Education in different fields leads to a multifaceted society with a wide range of professional backgrounds. A well-defined and forward-thinking education strategy is crucial for a country at the school and college levels since education leads to economic, political, and social advancement.

A new National Education Policy-2020 (NEP-2020) was launched thirty-four years after establishing the National Policy on Education in 1986. The new National Educational Policy 2020, published on July 29, 2020, seeks to establish and execute a slew of changes across all levels of education in India. Among other things, the NEP renamed the Ministry of Human Resource Development (MHRD) the Ministry of Education, Government of India, indicating the country's shift in emphasis toward education. The NEP-2020 vision is consistent with Goal 4 of the UN Sustainable Development Goals, which aspires to "provide inclusive and equitable quality education and encourage lifelong learning opportunities for everyone." The strategy is a comprehensive framework for elementary, secondary, and postsecondary education and vocational training in rural and urban India and intends to reform India's education sector.

Introduction

The new National Education Policy 2020 is the first education policy of the twenty-first century, and it attempts to address our country's numerous expanding developmental imperatives. This Policy proposes revising and revamping all aspects of the education structure, including regulation and governance, to replace it with a new system that is aligned with the aspirational goals of 21st-century education, including SDG4, while drawing on India's traditions and value systems. The New Education Policy asserts that India would become a worldwide knowledge superpower. It is also India-focused, with the goal of instilling "deep-rooted pride in being Indian" in the students. The deadline for meeting the goals, targets, and routes outlined by NEP-2020 is 2040.

Concepts

It is predicted that India will be the third largest economy in the world by 2030-2032, with estimated GDP of ten trillion dollars. It is obvious that the 10 trillion dollar economy will be powered by intellectual resources rather than the country's natural riches. The current administration intends to overhaul the Indian education industry by adopting a comprehensive National Education Policy 2020. This is consistent with Prime Minister Narendra Modi's recent push to capitalize on the Fourth Industrial Revolution to propel India to new heights. The recently proposed National Education Policy 2020 envisions an India-centered education system that, by offering high-quality education, actively contributes to our nation's long-term transformation into an egalitarian and thriving knowledge society.

Education is granted equal rights under the National Education Policy. It includes school education as an elementary component and makes it mandatory for all children. Multiple access and departure points have been provided for secondary students, and this extends to undergraduate, postgraduate, and research levels. It gives a student the freedom to finish his education whenever he wants. It was designed primarily for students who had to stop their studies in the middle due to employment or family obligations. The policy intends to provide a solid liberal arts foundation as well as vocational training at the undergraduate level. A candidate in the fourth year of an undergraduate programme can effortlessly integrate at the Masters and Doctoral levels, which will aid in the integration of professional education into mainstream undergraduate education in the long term. Vocational education will be included in the Education Policy as well.

The higher education sector has merged liberal arts with mathematics, sciences, technology, and engineering. The major goal of this is to build streamlined critical thinking, higher-order thinking, a better grasp of the subjects and domain, problem-solving abilities, as well as collaboration and communication skills. The postgraduate and doctoral levels now provide one-year, two-year, and five-year degree possibilities. The postgraduate programme will include more research-level topics as well as requirements for professional competence. The National Research Foundation was established with the primary goal of focusing on the Education System, primarily at the College and University levels. It will also be in charge of expanding research capacity and monitoring it through a more formal approach.

Digital literacy and computational thinking are the most significant components of this Education Policy. Students will be educated in programming and coding to improve their IT abilities, with an emphasis on making them digitally literate. NEP has been tasked with integrating ICT into education in order to make the process less onerous, faster, and more transparent. Through effective supervision, ICT would help pupils to receive a better education. NEP also intends to include online education into the educational process so that students may get the most out of their educational experience. The policy mentions incorporating disruptive technology into the system.

It will incorporate Artificial Intelligence and cognitive technologies to ensure that online education is directed by student learning and individual student improvement. It intends to build a massive IT infrastructure and technological platforms. It intends to offer an increasing number of online courses and anticipates collaborations with top-tier universities and institutes to offer additional Massive Open Online Courses (MOOCs).

Approaches to NEP 2020:

Curricular and Pedagogical Restructuring

It suggests replacing the present 10+2 pedagogical framework with a new structure of 5+3+3+4, with a solid foundation of Early Childhood Care and Education (ECCE) beginning at the age of three. The strategy calls for universal access to high-quality early childhood care and education with significant pedagogical components by 2030. It suggests that all students achieve fundamental literacy and numeracy (FLN) by third grade.

The fundamental focus of higher education structural reforms is to turn higher education institutions into massive interdisciplinary universities, colleges, and information centers.

Being multidisciplinary, institutions will rearrange their teaching, providing students with more subject options. It is also projected that associated colleges would eventually phase out, giving way to multidisciplinary universities and colleges by 2035.

The policy also advocates for the establishment of world-class interdisciplinary Higher Education

Institutions (HEIs) known as Multidisciplinary Educational Research Universities (MERU).

Teacher Availability and Training

The policy calls for a rethinking of the educational curriculum. However, in order to properly deliver the curriculum, schools and related authorities must train teachers and grasp the pedagogical requirements to ensure a seamless transition to the new education system. Furthermore, they must change the emphasis from teacher-centered to student-centered learning in order to encourage collaboration skills, critical thinking, problem-solving, and decision-making

capacities in young people. According to one study, approximately 250 million pupils are expected

to enroll in K-12 schools in India by 2030. This means that we will need approximately 7 million additional instructors to keep up with the growing student population. Teaching is one of the lowest-paid professions in India; thus, experiential learning and concept-oriented teaching would be difficult. The implementation of the NEP 2020 will be difficult until teacher compensation is altered.

Structure of Examination

The NEP emphasises formative rather than summative assessment for learning. The main goal of modifying the assessment system is to encourage ongoing tracking of learning outcomes. Continuous assessment, on the other hand, necessitates the deployment of novel evaluation methods and tasks by schools and instructors. These techniques need technology intervention and

teachers' and students' participation.

Use of Technology

The NEP 2020 emphasises the need of using technology to prepare youngsters for the future. However, establishing digital infrastructure such as digital classrooms, remote expertise-driven teaching models, AR/VR tools to bridge gaps in physical education, and laboratory infrastructure is a significant problem because most schools lack the necessary equipment to support these technologies. Furthermore, the expense of constructing digital infrastructure may be too expensive for all schools across the country.

Furthermore, in remote regions of the country where Internet access is scarce, employing digital learning tools is impossible. As a result, the government should focus on upgrading the fundamental infrastructure that will enable digital infrastructure in all domains. The new NEP 2020 proposes the formation of a National Educational Technology Forum (NETF) to serve as a forum for improving ideation, learning, evaluation, planning, and administration.

This policy seeks to ensure that technology is properly incorporated into all levels of education in order to improve teaching, learning, and assessment procedures, among other things.

School Education

Modification of the 10+2 structure to 5+3+3+4. Pre-primary years will be included in the new pedagogical and curricular structure. It's a positive departure because this was disregarded in education policy documents and only mentioned in passing. NCERT will concentrate on the creation of a new curricular and pedagogical structure for ECCE. Through short-term and long-term initiatives, the policy also dives deeply into the development and training of Anganwadi trainers. A positive push to formalise ECCE organisation and delivery. Priority should be given to achieving fundamental numeracy and reading by grade 3. The Ministry of Education (MoE) will enhance it and operate it as a separate national mission. A distinct national book policy to build libraries throughout the country and instill a love of reading in children. In India, public libraries are sparse. It would be beneficial if this could be enhanced through public education policy.

Mid-day lunches will be improved in terms of nutrition, with local options offered whenever feasible. Eggs remain a thorny policy topic; policy plays it safe by avoiding needless debate.

In collaboration with the Ministry of Social Justice and Empowerment, design programmes and initiatives to address the issue of dropouts. For some reason, the medium of teaching part has gained a lot of undue attention. However, in order to prevent any form of issue, the section stays quite flexible. This flexibility might have resulted from a shaky understanding, a commercial drive toward English, and a paternal concept of 'quality.' The policy also does not push/force/prefer one language over another and supports studying various languages. It also suggests teaching Korean, Japanese, Thai, French, German, Spanish, Portuguese, and Russian at the secondary level.

SEDGs are a new word introduced by policy (socio-economically disadvantaged groups). This has never been used as a social category in technical texts before. However, subsequent portions emphasise caste, ethnicity, handicap, and transgenders and make brief references to the word minority. Aside from technical critique, policy envisions several programmes aimed at these groups in order to enhance enrolment and retention. PARAKH, a new organisation focusing on exams such as the NAS (National Achievement Survey) and SAS (State Achievement Survey). PARAKH might be a useful tool for identifying learning gaps and assisting in the targeting of various ministry goals and activities.

Higher Education

It is critical to consider the policy from the perspective of what has been happening at public institutions, as well as the recent fiasco of eminent universities. The state has been gradually eroding university autonomy. Perverse state brutality launched on one of India's greatest public colleges did not occur in the distant past. Political appointments of university executives who, at best, serve as state tools rather than focusing on teaching, learning, research, or administration. Though the agreement emphasises regulatory autonomy, it would be concerning if it also implied financial autonomy. This 'imagined' autonomy is intended to be realised through the replacement of the UGC (University Grants Commission) and the AICTE (All India Council for Technical Education). The new Higher Education Commission of India is built on the concept of function separation and activity separation.

Policy also opposes the commercialization of education. However, in the same vein, international universities are welcome to visit India. Indian providers have significantly increased the number of private institutions. It would make sense if the goal was to increase competition. Inserting the statement, on the other hand, does not. Focusing on futuristic curricula makes sense, and establishing a distinct organisation committed to integrating technology into institutions is a vital step. Another excellent concept is the National Research Foundation. However, if these areas are occupied by persons with ideological goals, nothing can be anticipated. Indian universities would be able to establish campuses across the world, with a high potential for growth in gulf markets. The Indian diaspora has a high need for quality education.

Challenges

While the NEP has gained some momentum, the path to its implementation is littered with potholes.

1. The sheer size and variety of India's education industry make implementation difficult. Consider the scale of the school education system alone. India has the world's second-biggest education system, with over 15 lakh schools, 25 crore pupils, and 89 lakh instructors. The higher education system is also huge in scope. According to the AISHE 2019 report, 3.74 crore students are enrolled in roughly 1,000 universities, 39,931 colleges, and 10,725 stand-alone institutions in India's higher education system. As a result, nationwide implementation of this mega education policy will be a massive undertaking involving numerous stakeholders at the state, district, sub-district, and block levels. Creating a sense of shared responsibility and ownership among key stakeholders, including the corporate sector, at the state and district levels in areas of extreme variety will be a big challenge for education leaders.

2. The eventual realisation of the NEP is inextricably related to governmental capability. The NEP Drafting Committee, chaired by K. Kasturirangan, correctly said that India's education system is underfunded, overly bureaucratized, and lacks the potential for innovation and scale up. Internal capacities within education ministries (both central and state) and other regulatory agencies are woefully inadequate to guide the number of reforms envisioned in the NEP. Moving away from a rigid content-driven rote learning system to experiential learning and critical thinking, for example, would necessitate nothing less than a revolutionary shift in the attitudes of those in charge of the education system, let alone changes in the attitudes of teachers, students, and parents. This means that thousands of schools and colleges would require capacity building and reorientation in order to undertake a massive programme with several experiential goals. In summary, the ministry's current organisational structure and ecosystems will need to be completely overhauled. While the NEP document has laid out a comprehensive roadmap for overhauling the existing regulatory system, and the education ministry is in the process of bringing out legislation to facilitate the establishment of a Higher Education Commission of India (in place of existing regulatory bodies, primarily the UGC, AICTE, and National Council for Teachers Education), one must wait for the new institutional architecture to emerge out of his legislative initiative.

3. The NEP would be heavily reliant on the level of collaboration between the Centre and the states. While the Union government created the NEP (with participation from numerous stakeholders, including state governments), its execution is primarily dependent on the states' active involvement. This is because state governments are in charge of the majority of service-related education. In summary, the Centre must manage the ideals of cooperative federalism and decentralisation while implementing critical programmes. And with the recent deepening of political divisiveness and obvious breakdown of trust between the Centre and states, this is not an easy act to pull off. Many Opposition-ruled states have expressed significant opposition to several major aspects of the NEP and the way in which they are being implemented. The more concerning issue is that Tamil Nadu's recent decision not to adopt the NEP may inspire other Opposition-ruled states to follow suit. Thus, managing federal math is key to the NEP's realisation.

4. The business sector's participation, particularly in dealing with the higher education system, is important for realising the NEP's inclusionary agenda. It should be emphasised that the private sector operates up to 70% of higher education institutions (colleges and universities). Significantly, around 65-70 percent of current students are enrolled in private higher education institutions. Aside from that, the private sector contributes much-needed financial resources and innovation. As a result, it is critical for the government and regulatory organisations to develop appropriate institutional procedures to harness the private sector's participation and recognise it as an equal partner in the NEP process.

5. The successful implementation of significant initiatives necessitates the availability of enough financial resources over a long period of time. In this regard, the NEP declared that in order to achieve the aims of the new policy, the government must increase public spending on education to 6% of GDP. When one considers previous promises and their actual fulfillment, this is formidable endeavour. For example, the 1968 National Education Policy advocated allocating 6% of GDP to education. However, in all of these decades, state investment in education has never exceeded 3% of GDP. Ironically, the union budget allocation for education in the NEP's first year has decreased. The education budget was cut by 6%, from INR 99,311 crore in 2020-21 to INR 93,224 crore in 2021-22. While this is acceptable, given the government's priority in the face of the COVID-19 epidemic and the economic misery that vast parts of the people are experiencing, there is no clear plan for how such massive quantities of financial resources may be supplemented.

Conclusion

To conclude, the NEP 2020 is a really ground-breaking document in every way. Among other things, the strategy seeks to address pedagogical challenges, structural imbalances, and access expansion, as well as to prepare learners for the needs of a 21st-century India. At the same time, the NEP has the most difficult challenge of tackling several problems in the education system. Its successful implementation is crucial if India is to reap the demographic benefits and capitalise on the opportunities presented by a fast-developing knowledge economy. Given its revolutionary potential, the Centre has demonstrated urgency and a sense of purpose by undertaking a variety of activities in recent months, despite the pandemic's hurdles. Several states have formally started the policy, and several others are in the process of doing so. However, the NEP faces a difficult path ahead. Given its size and the level of complexity involved in its implementation, particularly guaranteeing coordination and collaboration among multiple stakeholders at the state, district, and private sector levels, it is a formidable task. Aside from that, one must contend with a lack of governmental capability, a lack of financial resources, and, most crucially, an education ecosystem that stifles fresh ideas and creativity. However, the most crucial difficulty facing the NEP is establishing an agreement and convincing states to take ownership of the first omnibus programme since 1986. In short, the NEP's effectiveness is primarily dependent on cooperative federalism and government ownership of the changes.

References

1. Kumar, K. (2005). Quality of Education at the Beginning of the 21st Century: Lessons from India.

2. Indian Educational Review Draft National Education Policy 2019,

3. National Education Policy 2020.

4. https://www.mhrd.gov.in/sites/upload_files/mhrd/files/nep/ NEP_Final_English.pdf

5. Yojana Magazine

6. https://innovate.mygov.in/wpcontent/uploads/2019/06/mygov15596510111.pdf

7. http://s3-ap-southeast-1.amazonaws.com/ijmer/pdf/volume10/volume10-issue2(5)/33.pdf

8. https://www.orfonline.org/expert-speak/five-challenges-that-would-shape-the-outcome-of-nep-2020/

9. https://digitallearning.eletsonline.com/2020/09/new-education-policy-2020-approaches-opportunities-and-challenges/

HOW NGOs GAINED MOMENTUM IN THE INDIAN EDUCATIONAL SECTOR

[1]BHUVNESH SONI, [2] AKANKSHA MALAVIA, [3]VANSHIKHA MAHANA, [4] ANUSHKA PARIHAR

[1,2,3]VICHAR SAMITI https://vicharsamiti.in/ INDIA
Email: [1]bhuvneshvrm@gmail.com , [2]akanksha.malaiya@gmail.com, [3]vanshikhamahana@gmail.com

The relevance and importance of education to the citizenry's and the country's overall social, economic, and political development has been continually the focus of international attention. This has particularly gained momentum with the development of the Millennium Development Goals (MDG). Research has shown that with improved literacy of the population, the political and economic circumstances of the country witnesses a massive improvement, the reason for this is fairly straight forward – a literate citizenry can meaningfully participate, partake and contribute to the economic development of the country.

In the Indian context, the education system can broadly be categorised into the government and the private school system. As per the Constitution of India, it is both the Central and the State Government that have the responsibility of ensuring improved accessibility of education in India. A country that permits both private and government schooling system faces multitude changes. The most prominent one being the distinction between the qualities of education offered by government and private schools. Owing to inadequacy of government funding, commitment, the quality of education in government schools take a hit. Meanwhile, students from private schools who come from affluent backgrounds continue to have access to the best of education that money can offer. Private schooling system in India witnessed a steady and steep growth since the 1990s when market reforms entered the educational sector.

It was this gap in the system that paved the way for NGOs intervention in the educational sector. Since the early 1960s, NGOs began focussing predominantly on education and health. NGOs not only directly participate in improving education through the setting up of schools and colleges, but also have a key role to play in conducting awareness camps and training programs for parents which inculcates the importance of primary and secondary education. Before stepping into a nuanced understanding of the work undertaken by NGOs in the education sector, a definitional understanding of NGOs must be provided. A Non-governmental organisation can be defined as one that is neither associated with the government nor is for the purpose of business, and profit making. NGOs are predominantly motivated by altruistic traits. The most interesting and efficient aspect of NGOs' working is that it provides for flexibility, and innovation in areas and manner of operation which helps alleviates real time concerns of individuals and communities.

In the educational sector, NGOs come in to provide effective support primarily for remote, rural schools. In the most remote and backward areas of the country, they come forward with provide access to primary and secondary education. However, the drawback is that NGOs are typically self-funded or privately funded and operate with limited resources. This prevents them from extending on a national and an international basis and they restrict areas of operation to specific pockets in the country. However, this trend has now shifted where NGOs are receiving financial and other non-financial aids by the government itself, or through large corporations. This has helped NGOs to significantly scale up their areas of operation.

In the Indian context, ever since the World Bank Report published as early as 2006, there were massive concerns regarding the quality of education, and the expectations that students and parents had with government run schools, particularly in rural India. Owing to population explosion, the foremost challenge has always been regarding rendering and ensuring quality education reaches the last child in the most remote and backward area of the country. Primarily, the challenges revolve around the lack of accountability and the absence of necessary infrastructure in government-run schools.

Unfortunately, despite India's abysmal performance on several educational rankings, there has been negligible government effort to change the existing scenario. Year after year, government budgetary allocation towards the education sector remains the same. Research indicates that over 180 million children are taught by almost 5.7 million teachers in more than 1.2 million primary and upper primary schools across the country. As a natural corollary to this, research undertaken by several prominent organisations indicate that learning outcomes in government-run primary schools is disappointing and below the bare minimum acceptable levels. In addition to this, the quality of education across these government-run schools differ based on the location of the said schools. The Annual Status of Education Report conducted since 2005 indicates that across all rural districts situated in India, only 53% of Class V students in rural India could read a textbook that belonged with Grade II students. In addition to this, only 36% of students were in a position to successfully solve three digit by one digit division problem. The understanding that one gains from this is that, unfortunately, a large majority of students in government run schools lack very basic skills that students of their age typically possess.

The foremost identifiable cause for this is that teaching methods that is predominantly and primarily employed in primary schools are focused upon recitation and memorisation of textbook materials. In this backdrop, the role of the teacher is limited or reduced to just monitor the maintenance of decorum in classrooms and schools. As early as 2005, the Government of India had taken cognisance of this downward trend and had suggested multiple approaches to improving learning outcomes. In so far as the NGO context is concerned, it was suggested that teachers, particularly those in primary school based out of rural areas be made aware of existing NGO initiatives.

What one can gather from the aforementioned data is that school curriculum is in need of a massive revamp, and there is a lack of quality teaching facilities in India. To be fair, to some extent, the government has attempted improvements through the Right to Education route as it directly addresses several deficiencies stated and discussed in the preceding paragraphs.

However, improvement in the overall educational system of the country would require intervention at the local and community level. It is at this stage that government participation is limited, and NGO participation becomes the key.

An international report remarks that NGOs have taken on the role of being the main service providers in countries such as India where the government has failed in fulfilling its traditional mandate on education. Previously, NGOs were focused only upon undertaking –gap-filling" initiatives, but have now moved forward and stepped into innovation and capacity building as well.

An inspiring story is that of Rishi Valley Institute for Educational Resources which was based out of Andhra Pradesh in India. Ironically, although the state of Andhra is famously known for its IT boom and development, the economic and social disparities between the rural and the urban areas were shockingly disappointing. Nearly 49% of schools in the state of Andhra Pradesh have an enrolment of 50 students or fewer. In addition to this, the average primary school enrolment in 87 students. The Rishi Valley Education Centre was established as early as 1931 and located in Chittoor District of the state of Andhra Pradesh. The area of operation of the NGO was one of the most remote and drought hit area in southern India. The focus of the NGO was to organise, expand and improvise rural education programme that was being offered in the area. The problems that were being faced and countered by school students in the area revolved around the quality of education and manner of management of rural, locally run schools. The foremost problem was regarding the small size of the settlement which meant that the government typically shied away establishing a larger school with sufficient infrastructure. The rationale provided was that the small number of students enrolled in the school would not justify expanding budgetary allocations to the said school. However, subsequently, the NGO received government funding from the Department of Education, Government of India to develop and alternative model of education. The objective was to address existing problems in these schools. The NGO focused on developing a child-centric model of education. This was in consultation with key stakeholders such as the rural students themselves, their parents and teachers who were currently involved in schooling activities.

Research undertaken a year into the establishment of this alternative model of education and schooling revealed that there was a significant and large-scale decrease in the dropout rates among school going children. In addition to this, it was also observed that the number of students who passed had significantly improved. Pursuant to this observation, a study was conducted to look into the methodology adopted by the NGO to determine whether it is a sustainable model that can be developed all across India. Interestingly, it was revealed that the manner of design of school curriculum was centred around appropriate language used which consider and factored into local traditions, customs, and the requirement of the community at large. In addition to this, as studies revealed a huge gap in the learning abilities of students, the NGO shifted its model of education and curriculum; from merely texts and words, to pictures and photographs being included in the course of study.

The aforementioned had validated the role, significance and importance of NGOs in the educational sector. Their role is indispensable particularly in the context of universalising elementary and primary school education in India. In addition to improving the overall holistic accessibility of education in rural India, education has also played a key role in developing cost-effective approaches to education in the form of decentralised system. NGO intervention had brought to the fore multi-grade, multi-level teaching, child-centric policies to the fore. In addition to this, it has also enhanced classroom participation and efficaciousness of study outcomes. Therefore, they play a crucial role in strengthening and putting forward the goals and aspirations of the state.

However, while highlighting the importance of a robust NGO network in expanding educational reach, we must also take into cognisance the inherent limitations of the NGO model. The foremost being limited participation of NGOs, although NGOs have been growing in number, scale and reach, considering the sheer volume of requirement in a country like India, NGO participation continues to be negligible. It is of utmost importance that we recognise that the NGOs cannot possibly operate as a parallel provider of education, and the government run model of schooling continue to be the model of sustainability. Further, even in circumstances wherein collaborative opportunities arise, it is typically in the context of reaching education to the most remote and backward areas, however, in the context of NGO consultation for broad consultative role, their involvement is fairly limited. NGOs are often sceptical of governmental aid and assistance owing to vagaries of their policies and directives. They fear that decades of good work may amount to nothing owing to sudden shift in governmental policies and considerations.

Furthermore, NGOs operate in a specified geographical location which inherently has the effect of limiting their activities and reach. Therefore, they aid the government in terms of implementation of goals and policies at the micro, and community level. This means that larger macro aspirations continue to fall within the realm of governmental operation. However, recently we see an optimistic trend where not only have NGOs been able to scale their activities, but we see a consistent adoption of NGO model in education by several government organisations. It is of utmost importance that clear strategic institutional alliances be built for NGOs to scale up their activities. In addition to this, governmental departments are increasing involving NGOs in their consultative and policy frameworks. It is at this juncture that NGOs have been able to put forward their viewpoints, experiences, and expertise. The foremost example of this would be when the NCERT invited consultations with NGOs in its initiative for revising the national curriculum framework for the primary years.

In addition to increasing the reach and accessibility of education, it is equally important that there be a quality check on the content of syllabus and curriculum. The need of the hour in the educational sector is upon enhanced professional support and training in addition to motivating the teaching and non-teaching staff. It is not merely sufficient that governmental expenditure is focused upon physical infrastructure of schools. It is equally important that investments in teachers and their education and training is made a top-most priority.

In addition to this, focus must be laid on analysing and understanding the alternative school model and para teachers. It is of utmost importance that there is larger political consensus and commitment towards greater investments in these models of schooling. Survey has revealed the importance of non-formalisation of the formal schools which is said to have the positive impacts of making education flexible and responsive. In addition to this, it is also important that NGOs parallel work with a wider constituency within the existing governmental framework. Expansion of NGO activities must be undertaken keeping in mind existing governmental and societal framework in India. Further, an developing an internal NGO mission and vision is sine qua non to the effective, efficacious and efficient working on the NGO system as regards the educational section. This vision and mission must then be shared with governmental organisations in order to collaborate on shared platforms and ideologies.

In addition to this, with due consideration to the limitation of NGO activities in terms of the area and scope, it is of utmost importance that NGOs organise within themselves. This would provide a forum for continuous advocacy and social audit and the utility of this cannot be overstated. The operation of NGOs can work in a hierarchical manner with bigger, better-funded NGOs leading the way through partnering with NGOs which have a more limited reach. However, NGO operation in isolation is hardly ever useful. It is important that the work of the NGOs take part in a collaborative environment at all levels including the national, state, district, and taluk levels. NGOs can partner with others working in the same sector and share experiences and knowledge amongst themselves. This could also potentially pave the way for joint advocacy of several NGOs which would, by default, have the effect of expanding the reach, size, and scope of each NGO operation.

In so far as the education sector is concerned, particularly considering the post-pandemic world, the importance of technological interventions cannot be overstated. It is of utmost importance that NGOs collaborate with local, national and international organisations in order to consistently upgrade their technical competencies and abilities. Furthermore, so far, NGOs predominantly consult the Central and the concerned state government in so far as their operation is concerned. However, considering their direct impact at the grass-roots level, it is important to ensure that there is coordinated support mechanism that is provided by the locally elected governments. This may be in the form and manner of a joint vision building exercise this would automatically expand the scope and well-being of these non-governmental organisations.

NGO resources should be drawn upon by external agencies for technical backstopping and monitoring. There have been instances of NGOs forming part of Technical Support Groups, which need to be further supported, mainly in a way that protects ongoing collaborative endeavours from the vagaries of official policy. As NGOs are assigned increasingly larger roles, an accountability framework for NGO action, which balances the need for NGO autonomy with responsibility towards the Government, needs to be built. NGO personnel should be called upon for reviews and supervision. Research, documentation, evaluation and social audits by NGOs should be built into the external agency programs

Further, funding is an aspect of critical concern for the establishment and sustenance of these non-governmental organisations. It is important that financing be ensured either through large corporate organisations or via governmental budgetary allocations. As innovations and expertise of these organisations mature, it is important that they be regularly and continually funded through regular budgetary allocations. A cross-section of experts could be called upon in order to meaningfully and fruitfully identify and list organisations which are undertaking extensive work in the educational sector. With these suggestions being made, the participation and involvement of the civil section of the society cannot be overstated. Ultimately, governmental involvement and mutual collaborative framework amongst the NGOs themselves can only go so far in the absence of support of the general public in the country. One of the most effective ways to ensure participative rights of the general public is through seeking people's feedback. This would provide genuine insight into grass-roots level impressions and perceptions.

VOTE OF THANKS

It is expressed with the deepest and utmost gratitude to all the people who have been an indispensable part of this book and made a crucial contribution towards the completion of this book which is very near and dear to us. We are very grateful for the hard work with which all of you put your efforts in. This task could not have been possible without the sheer determination, assiduous, and diligent work of all the people involved in this task. Thank you to each one of you towards the successful accomplishment of this tremendous task.

****

www.ingramcontent.com/pod-product-compliance
Ingram Content Group UK Ltd.
Pitfield, Milton Keynes, MK11 3LW, UK
UKHW050904070225
4473UKWH00035B/731